Cottages

Somewhere is better than anywhere.

—Flannery O'Connor

somewhere beyond the sea...

Cottages

Charming Seaside & Tidewater Designs

The Sater Design Collection

HOME PLANNERS
TUCSON, ARIZONA

Published by Home Planners
A Division of Hanley-Wood, Inc.
Editorial and Corporate Offices:
3275 West Ina Road, Suite 110
Tucson, Arizona 85741

Distribution Center:
29333 Lorie Lane
Wixom, Michigan 48393

Rickard D. Bailey, CEO and Publisher
Cindy Coatsworth Lewis, Publications Manager
Jan Prideaux, Senior Editor

Editor Laura Hurst Brown

Designer Matthew S. Kauffman

Illustrated by Jenkins & Chin Shue, Boca Raton

First Printing, January, 1998

10 9 8 7 6 5 4 3 2 1

Printed in the United States of America
Library of Congress Catalog Card Number: 97-077459
ISBN softcover: 1-881955-46-X

beyond the moon and stars...

Contents

there's a place

Introduction

Imagine a cottage infused with the whimsical spirit of a tropical paradise—a dreamy refuge that calls to mind a place as timeless as the sea itself. The Sater Design Collection presents a new breed of home designs perfectly suited to casual living, as inviting in the hills of New England as on the shores of a Caribbean island—or nestled in the bluffs of Malibu.

Inspired by Southern island-community cottages, Dan F. Sater II envisioned a fresh architecture that would preserve the region's rich heritage but add a vibrant aesthetic. Contemporary, high-pitched rooflines, seaside porticos and hosts of French doors create an air of casual elegance, while vintage 19th-century details add a sense of rich comfort. Stunning sunbursts and stately towers set off grand porticos and sheltered verandahs, and almost every room offers a picture-perfect view.

Careful to embrace the traditional vernacular, Dan adapted historic visual elements and tactile qualities to fit modern tastes. This collection reflects a unique blend of Southern Cracker, Key West Conch, Louisiana Creole, Nantucket and Bahamian flavors—all dressed with a grand simplicity. Each design's playful geometry exhibits a sense of time and place drawn from Old Charleston Row and Caribbean plantation houses and translates it to a diverse identity ready for any region.

The lively forms and high-spirited lines of Sater's cottages honor the past but are well-fixed with a comfortable vocabulary of their own. Traditional arrangements convert to flexible interiors and high style softens to relaxed spaces designed to ease the demands of every-day living. Getting away from it all can be much more than a mere flight of fancy—with sun-drenched decks and moonlit verandahs, it can be a different way of life.

where dreams are made.

820
Mallory Square

© The Sater Group, Inc.

W elcome home to casual, unstuffy living with this comfortable tidewater design. Asymmetrical lines celebrate the turn of the new century, and blend a current Gulf Coast style with vintage chic brought forward from its regional past. A glass-paneled entry is announced by a hooded pediment and set off by a sunburst transom.

The foyer overlooks a decorative half-wall to wide views offered through French doors. The heart of this home is the great room, where a put-your-feet-up atmosphere prevails, and the dusky hues of sunset can mingle with the sounds of ocean breakers. A galley-style kitchen serves an eating bar, while a convenient pass-through offers magnificent views to the cook.

The center vestibule leads to a laundry and a full bath, and to a secondary bedroom or study with a large, front-facing window. French doors open the master suite to a private area of the covered porch, where sunlight and sea breezes mingle with a spirit of *bon vivant*.

Plan 6691

Total Living Area: 1,288 square feet
Price Schedule: C
Width 32'-4"
Depth 60'-0"

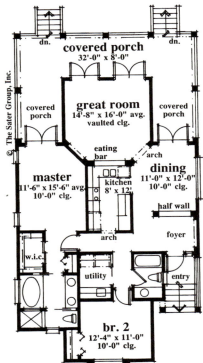

© The Sater Group, Inc.

covered porch
32'-0" x 8'-0"

dn.   dn.

covered porch

great room
14'-8" x 16'-0" avg.
vaulted clg.

covered porch

eating bar

arch

master
11'-6" x 15'-6" avg.
10'-0" clg.

kitchen
8' x 12'

dining
11'-0" x 12'-0"
10'-0" clg.

half wall

foyer

w.i.c.

arch

utility

entry

br. 2
12'-4" x 11'-0"
10'-0" clg.

A gentle Caribbean flavor warms this Gulf Coast design, rich with details cultivated from the past. Lose track of time in a cozy, comfortable interior that invites year-round living.

© The Sater Group, Inc.

Rear Perspective

163
Georgetown Cove

© The Sater Group, Inc.

The Sater Design Collection

The captivating charm of this popular cottage calls up a sense of gentler times, with a quaint front balcony, horizontal siding and fishscale shingles. A contemporary, high-pitched roof harmonizes with sunbursts and double porticos, while a glass-paneled entry opens to the foyer, where a straight-forward staircase leads to a bright vestibule.

In the great room, lovely French doors bring the outside in, and a fireplace framed by built-in cabinetry adds coziness and warmth. A gourmet kitchen sports an island counter with a prep sink, and a peninsular counter with a casual eating bar. The formal dining room opens to a private area of the covered porch—an elegant invitation to dining outdoors.

Double French doors and circlehead windows fill the upper-level master suite with sunlight and open to a private sundeck. The nearby study, or spare bedroom, features its own walk-in closet and views to the side property. Bedroom 2 resides off the mid-level landing and has its own full bath.

Plan 6690

Main Level: 876 square feet

Upper Level: 948 square feet

Total Living Area: 1,824 square feet

Price Schedule: C

Width 27'-6"

Depth 64'-0"

The columned verandah sets a quaint, romantic pace for this homey river cottage. Sultry, tropical breezes flow in and out of the cozy, comfortable interior through a host of French doors.

© The Sater Group, Inc.

Rear Perspective

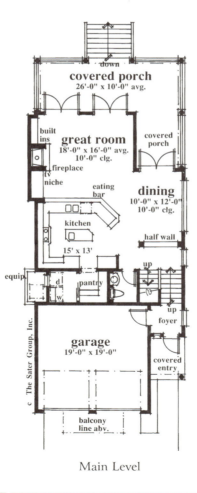

Main Level

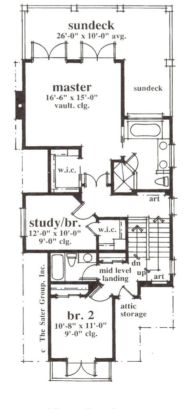

Upper Level

552
Periwinkle Way

© The Sater Group, Inc.

A romantic air flirts with the clean, simple lines of this seaside getaway, set off by stunning shingle accents and a sunburst transom. Horizontal siding complements an insulated metal roof to create a charming look that calls up a sense of 19th-century style. Inside, an unrestrained floor plan harbors cozy interior spaces and offers great outdoor views through wide windows and French doors.

At the heart of the home, the two-story great room features a corner fireplace, an angled entertainment center and an eating bar shared with the gourmet kitchen. Columns and sweeping archways define the formal dining room, while French doors open to the verandah, inviting dreamy ocean breezes inside.

The main-level master suite provides a relaxing bath with a garden tub, a windowed shower and two lavatories. Upstairs, an expansive deck captures panoramic views and serves the sounds of the sea to a secondary bedroom which shares a bath with Bedroom 3. A gallery hall offers a balcony overlook with interior vistas to the great room.

Plan 6683

Main Level: 1,290 square feet

Upper Level: 548 square feet

Total Living Area: 1,838 square feet

Price Schedule: D

Width 38'-0"

Depth 51'-0"

Old South comfort and modern style balance past and present with this engaging plan. History-rich details lovingly rethink tradition to create a new notion of home.

© The Sater Group, Inc.

Rear Perspective

Main Level

covered porch
18'-0" x 10'-0"

master
13'-0" x 15'-0"
vaulted clg.

corner fireplace

entertainment center

w.i.c.

great room
16'-0" x 18'-0"
2 story clg.

dining
11'-0" x 13'-0"
8'-0" clg.

arch

eating bar

arch

arch

butlers pantry

kitchen

foyer

storage

10' x 16'

w'd

covered entry porch

up

down

© The Sater Group, Inc.

Upper Level

deck
18'-0" x 10'-0"

open to grand room below

br. 2
10'-6" x 11'-6"
vaulted clg.

overlook

attic storage access door

arch

br. 3
10'-0" x 12'-0"
vaulted clg.

down

© The Sater Group, Inc.

622

Charleston Street

© The Sater Group, Inc.

Louvered shutters, balustered railings and a slate-style roof complement a stucco-and-siding blend and call up the Row-house style, infused with a tropical flavor. Breezes whisper through plantation-style galleries, which help define a new look that marries past and present. Interior spaces that are long on views achieve a narrow footprint, perfect for slender lots.

Entry stairs lead to the main-level living areas, defined by arches and columns that blend Old World craftsmanship with modern space. A wall of built-ins and a warming fireplace redefine the open, contemporary great room with a cozier dimension. Four sets of French doors expand the living area to the gallery and extends an invitation to gentle afternoon breezes.

Upper-level sleeping quarters include a guest suite with a bayed sitting area, an additional bedroom and a full bath. The master suite features separate vanities, private water closet and shower areas, and a tray ceiling. French doors lead to a private deck, which offers a "sit and look at the stars" vantage point.

Balusters, shutters and French doors contribute to the British Colonial influence of this design.

Plan 6700

Main Level: 1,305 square feet

Upper Level: 1,215 square feet

Total Living Area: 2,520 square feet

Bonus Space: 935 square feet

Price Schedule: D

Width 30'-6"

Depth 72'-2"

sun-kissed decks play harmony to wraparound porticos with this modern Row house. Toss a splendid party—alfresco, of course, in the garden courtyard.

© The Sater Group, Inc.

Rear Perspective

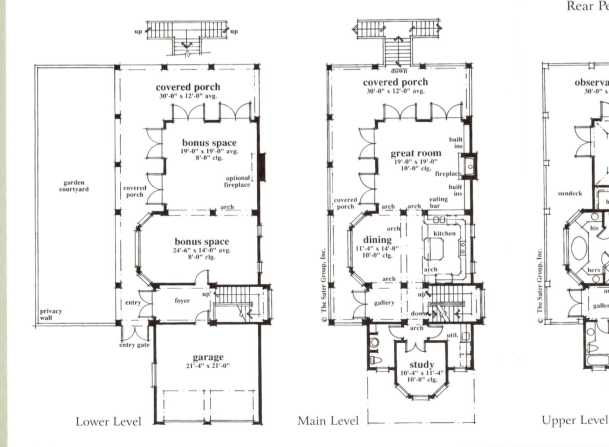

Lower Level

Main Level

Upper Level

756
Church Street

© The Sater Group, Inc.

The modest detailing of Greek Revival style gave rise to this grand cottage, rich with architectural character. A mid-level foyer eases the trip from ground level to the raised living area, while an arched vestibule announces the great room. French doors flank the heart of the home, adding views as well as a sense of whimsy.

The formal dining room opens through a dropped arch soffit ceiling, and French doors lead to the covered porch. Fixed glass windows above the built-in cabinetry allow views and natural light to fill the great room. A well-appointed kitchen enjoys generous views and serves a casual eating bar as well as the dining room.

Upstairs, each of two private suites has a windowed tub, a vanity and wardrobe space. A pair of French doors opens each of the bedrooms to an observation sundeck through covered porches. The upper gallery hall leads to a computer loft with built-ins and a balcony overlook.

Plan 6687

Main Level: 942 square feet

Upper Level: 571 square feet

Total Living Area: 1,513 square feet

Lower Level Entry: 167 square feet

Price Schedule: C

Width 32'-0"

Depth 53'-0"

Period charm and classic formality embrace an impromptu spirit and a "lose the shoes" attitude with this Revival home. On a clear day, you may see forever from the stunning sundeck.

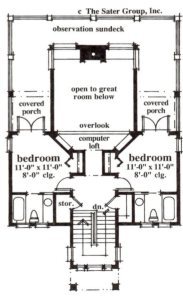

© The Sater Group, Inc

Rear Perspective

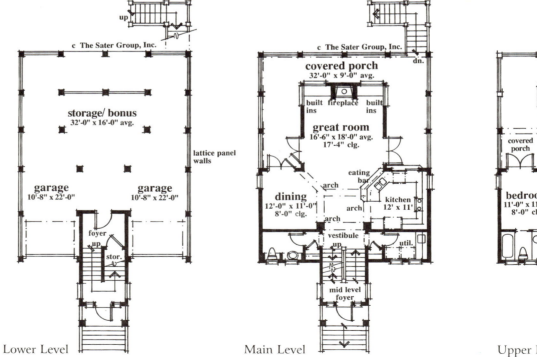

Lower Level

Main Level

Upper Level

924
Shadow Lane

© The Sater Group, Inc.

The captivating island of Key West has inspired a host of comfortable styles that invite ocean breezes to travel freely from front to back. This cozy retreat pays homage to that vintage spirit with living areas that are light and airy, and covered porches that offer long vistas of sun-washed beaches.

Built-ins and a media niche frame the fireplace in the great room, creating a cozy complement to views of prize sunsets and luxuriant moonlight. Shoes may be strictly optional, even in the formal dining room, which opens to the wraparound covered porch. The gourmet kitchen serves both casual and planned events, and shares an eating bar with the great room. A secondary bedroom on this level has access to a full bath.

The second level is dedicated to the master suite, where the bedwall faces the private observation deck—a perfect spot for morning coffee. A sensible bath offers a U-shape walk-in closet, an oversize shower and a compartmented toilet. A vestibule leads to a viewing-loft stair and to Bedroom 3, where a built-in window seat may be strewn with beach quilts and comfy ticking pillows.

Plan 6686

Main Level: 1,046 square feet
Upper Level: 638 square feet
Total Living Area: 1,684 square feet
Price Schedule: C
Width 25'-0"
Depth 65'-6"

sun-drenched observation decks command knock-out views with this Caribbean-style home. Arches, columns and French doors lend a gentle European flavor that's the last word in seaside retreats.

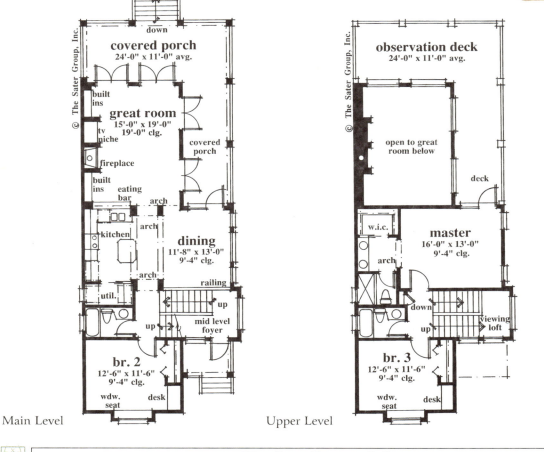

Rear Perspective

© The Sater Group, Inc.

Main Level

Upper Level

113
Bridgeport Harbour

© The Sater Group, Inc.

The Sater Design Collection

Jamaican plantation houses inspired this cottage design, lovingly revived by the Old Charleston Row homes. Vintage details speak softly of a Southern heritage but defy the past with hard-working amenities and easy, open spaces that invite the future. A study in contrasts, the home mixes refined craftsmanship with definitive creature comforts. Arched columns define both formal and casual spaces, for an engaging, easygoing theme that flows throughout the well-lit interior.

Wraparound porticos on two levels offer seaside views to the living areas, while an observation deck for stargazing opens from the master suite. Four sets of French doors bring the outside in to the great room. Fling them wide open and let the crackle of the fireplace play harmony to the soft sounds of the sea.

The upper-level master suite features a spacious bath designed for two. Three sets of doors open to the observation deck with a special place for sunning. A guest bedroom on this level leads to a gallery hall with its own access to the deck. Generous bonus space awaits development on the lower level, which—true to its Old Charleston roots—opens gloriously to a garden courtyard.

Plan 6685

Main Level: 1,305 square feet

Upper Level: 1,215 square feet

Total Living Area: 2,520 square feet

Bonus Space: 935 square feet

Price Schedule: D

Width 30'-6"

Depth 72'-2"

This elegant Old Charleston Row design blends high vogue with a restful character that says shoes are definitely optional. A flexible interior enjoys modern space that welcomes sunlight.

Rear Perspective

© The Sater Group, Inc.

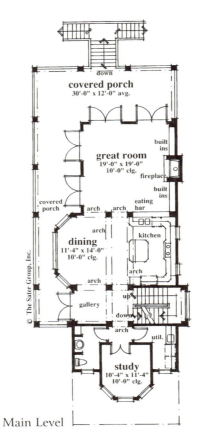

Lower Level

Main Level

Upper Level

909
Duval Street

The Sater Design Collection

Key West Conch style blends Old World charm with New World comfort in this picturesque design. A glass-paneled entry lends a warm welcome and complements a captivating front balcony. The balanced floor plan works well within a narrow footprint—reminiscent of the Caribbean "shotgun" houses.

Two sets of French doors open the great room to wide views and extend the living areas to the back covered porch. A gourmet kitchen is prepared for any occasion with a prep sink, plenty of counter space, an ample pantry and an eating bar. The mid-level landing leads to two additional bedrooms, a full bath and a windowed art niche.

Double French doors open the upper-level master suite to a sundeck and offer powerful views from the bedroom. Circle-head windows and a vaulted ceiling maintain a light and airy atmosphere. The master bath has a windowed soaking tub and a glass-enclosed walk-in shower. Sunsets may be viewed from the privacy of the deck, a remarkable vantage point in moonlight as well. The plan offers the option of a fourth bedroom.

Plan 6701

Main Level: 876 square feet

Upper Level: 1,245 square feet

Total Living Area: 2,123 square feet

Price Schedule: C

Width 27'-6"

Depth 64'-0"

Double porticos and sunburst transoms dress up this Key West Conch plan. Round columns define the verandah, while crafted details unify the living levels with room for growth and guests.

© The Sater Group, Inc.

Rear Perspective

Main Level

covered porch
26'-0" x 10'-0" avg.

built ins

great room
18'-0" x 16'-0" avg.
10'-0" clg.

covered porch

fireplace

tv niche

eating bar

dining
10'-0" x 12'-0"
10'-0" clg.

kitchen

15' x 13'

half wall

up

equip

d w

pantry

up

foyer

garage
19'-0" x 19'-0"

covered entry

balcony line abv.

c The Sater Group, Inc.

Upper Level

sundeck
26'-0" x 10'-0" avg.

master
16'-6" x 15'-0"
vault. clg.

sundeck

w.i.c.

art

study/br.
12'-0" x 10'-0"
9'-0" clg.

w.i.c.

dn.

landing

up

art

br. 2
9'-8" x 11'-0"
9'-0" clg.

br. 3
9'-8" x 11'-0"
9'-0" clg.

700
Cayman Court

© The Sater Group, Inc.

A charming porte-cochere sets off a perfect blend of Southern Cracker comfort and Gulf Coast style with this sea-side retreat. Exposed rafters, lattice panels and a deep covered porch make a strong architectural statement that's tuned to a 1940s personality. Ocean breezes flow under as well as through the raised living area, which rallies a full palette of living spaces within a modest footprint.

The covered entry porch runs the width of the home, creating an outdoor haven for cozy family gatherings and leisurely chats with neighbors. Inside, decorative arches and columns make a grand entrance to the living and dining areas. The gourmet kitchen provides a pass-through to the formal dining room, while a focal-point fireplace warms the great room.

A secluded master suite nestles to the back of the plan, with private access to a sundeck and French doors to the covered porch. The bayed sitting area offers space for reading and sunlight to the homeowner's retreat. His and Hers walk-in closets provides plenty of storage, while a garden soaking tub enjoys a bright, bumped-out bay in the master bath. The plan includes pier and crawlspace foundation options.

Plan 6694

Total Living Area: 1,792 square feet
Price Schedule: C
Width 32'-0"
Depth 82'-0"

© The Sater Group, Inc.

Rear Perspective

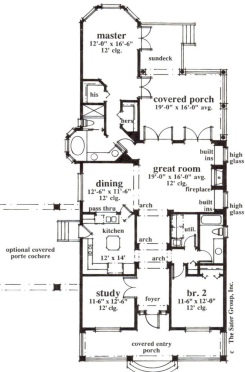

This seaside getaway is infused with the gracious spirit of the Louisiana Creole style. A wide porch with deep overhangs encourages lingering, even in sultry weather.

138
Jasmine Lane

© The Sater Group, Inc.

An enchanting center gable announces a graceful, honest architecture that's at home with the easygoing nature of this coastal design. A columned porch and romantic fretwork lend balance and proportion outside, while gentle arches add pleasing definition to an open interior that enjoys a modern sense of space.

The well-appointed kitchen features a corner walk-in pantry, an eating bar for easy meals, and an angled double sink. A box bay fills the dining room with light and allows space for a china hutch or buffet. French doors in the main-level secondary bedroom lead to a covered balcony with views of the front property.

The foyer stairs lead to second-level sleeping quarters, which include a master suite with a spacious bedroom and a lavish private bath. A gallery hall with a balcony overlook to the great room leads to an additional bedroom with its own full bath.

Enjoy lofty views from the comfort of a chaise longue in the quiet sitting area of the stair tower. The plan includes pier and crawlspace foundation options.

Plan 6680

Main Level: 1,007 square feet

Upper Level: 869 square feet

Total Living Area: 1,876 square feet

Price Schedule: D

Width 43'-8"

Depth 53'-6"

A Caribbean-style tower rises above this hip-roof coastal cottage like a fairy-tale castle turret. Dreamy views and French doors define an open interior and blend new traditions with those of the past.

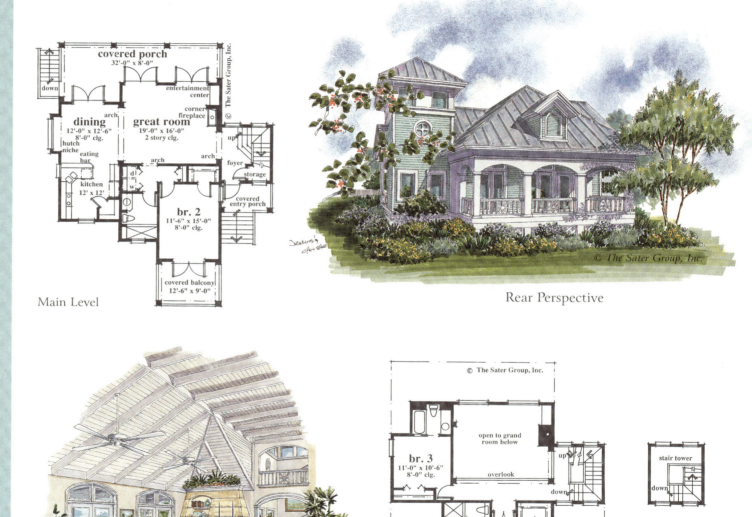

Main Level

Rear Perspective

Upper Level

841

Saddle River

© The Sater Group, Inc.

Lattice fretwork and symmetrical gables create a pure geometry on this easy-living river cottage, while a stair tower adds a sense of grandeur. A host of French doors on the main level invites the outside in, where an air of comfortable elegance prevails. The great room features a vaulted ceiling and opens to a central gallery, defined by graceful arches.

Both the formal dining room, the gallery and the great room open through sets of lovely French doors to the columned verandah. Traditional events, such as holidays, will enjoy an unstuffy atmosphere in joyful rooms that lead outdoors and invite a sense of nature. Wrapping counters in the gourmet kitchen surround an island counter large enough for two cooks.

Sleeping quarters upstairs include the spacious master suite, which opens to a private balcony where gentle sea breezes can invigorate the senses. Indoors, a convenient morning kitchen serves juice and coffee. An additional bedroom on this level employs a hall bath with built-in shelves. A wrapping staircase leads up to a tower loft and observation deck.

Plan 6681

Main Level: 906 square feet

Upper Level: 714 square feet

Lower Level Entry: 86 square feet

Total Living Area: 1,706 square feet

Price Schedule: D

Width 40'-0"

Depth 37'-0"

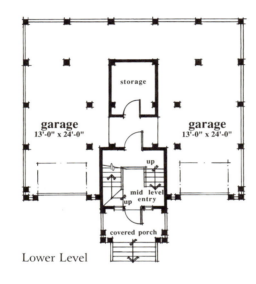

Lower Level

© The Sater Group, Inc.

Rear Perspective

The dramatic stair tower plays harmony to the balanced symmetry of this river cottage. An observation deck offers a place to gaze seaward to where the world falls away.

Main Level

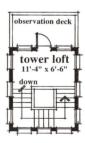

Upper Level

462
Savannah Sound

© The Sater Group, Inc.

Stunning New South charm flavors this joyful reinterpretation of Key West island style. Asymmetrical rooflines set off a grand turret and a two-story bay that allows glorious views within. Cottage charm gives way to urbane comforts through the covered entry, with a mid-level foyer to ease the way.

Glass doors open the great room to a sun-kissed deck, while arch-top clerestory windows enhance the casual atmosphere with natural light. A corner fireplace and a wetbar create warmth and coziness in the living and dining rooms. The gourmet kitchen boasts a center island with an eating bar for easy meals, plus a windowed wrapping counter.

A winding staircase leads to a luxurious upper-level master suite that opens to a private master balcony, while a morning kitchen offers juice and coffee service. A two-sided fireplace warms both the bedroom and a bath designed for two. The gallery hall has a balcony overlook and leads to a secluded study, which enjoys wide views through a front bay window.

Plan 6698

Main Level: 1,684 square feet

Upper Level: 1,195 square feet

Total Living Area: 2,879 square feet

Price Schedule: D

Width 45'-0"

Depth 52'-0"

Beautiful windows and columned verandahs set off the rear vista and capture natural light and seaside views. An eclectic style adds Southern charm to a tropical flavor.

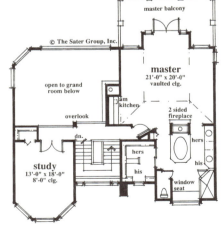

© The Sater Group, Inc.

Rear Perspective

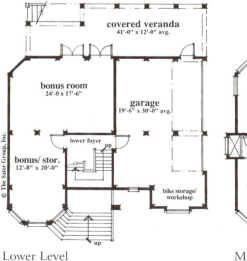

Lower Level

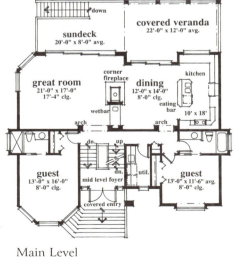

Main Level

Upper Level

404
Hemingway Lane

© The Sater Group, Inc.

The Sater Design Collection

Prevailing summer breezes find their way through many joyful rooms in this Neoclassical Revival home. Inspired by 19th-century Key West island houses, the 21st-century facade is heart-stoppingly beautiful with Doric columns and a glass-paneled, arched entry. The mid-level foyer eases the trip from ground level to living and dining areas, which offer flexible space for planned events or cozy gatherings.

Two sets of French doors lead out to the gallery and sundeck, and a two-story picture window invites natural light and a spirit of *bon vivant* to pour into the heart of the home. A dreamy, oversized kitchen has a walk-in pantry, a food preparation island and its own French door to the covered porch.

In the main-level master suite, French doors capture generous views and open to the covered porch. Upper-level sleeping quarters include four bedrooms which take full advantage of their lofty placement. Bedrooms 2 and 3 each open to a private covered balcony with a sun-kissed deck, while two shared baths have dormered showers. A central computer loft offers built-in desk space and a balcony overlook.

PLAN 6689

Main Level: 1642 square feet

Upper Level: 1,165 square feet

Lower Level Entry: 150 square feet

Total Living Area: 2,957 square feet

Price Schedule: D

Width 44'-6"

Depth 58'-0"

Traditional warmth surrounds the flow of modern life in this Key West design. Paneled windows allow panoramic views and lend a sense of unity to an eclectic theme.

© The Sater Group, Inc.

Rear Perspective

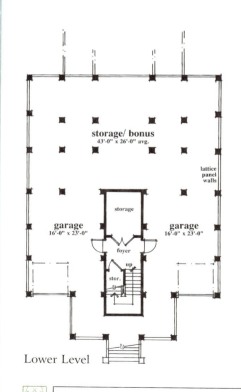

Lower Level

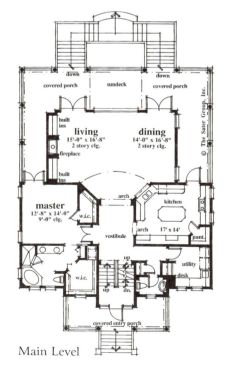

Main Level

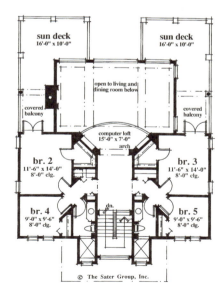

Upper Level

624
Seagrove Beach

Bright colors set off this historic but perfectly contemporary facade, enhanced by a romantic bay rich with sunburst transoms. Key West island classics inspired a high-pitched metal roof and rear porticos decked with balusters, columns and an arched truss.

A light and airy interior opens to the covered verandah through sliding glass and French doors. The great room hosts a corner fireplace and an island entertainment center, and brings in spectacular views through walls of glass. In a perfect arrangement for entertaining, the formal dining room opens to both the great room and the gourmet kitchen.

A main-level gallery hall leads to a secluded study which enjoys its own access to the covered verandah. At the other side of the plan, a convenient powder room maintains privacy for a guest suite that takes full advantage of the bay windows. Upstairs, the master suite features a private balcony and sundeck, a well lit bath and a separate room for computers and books. A gallery loft with a balcony overlook leads to a second guest suite.

Plan 6682

Main Level: 1,617 square feet

Upper Level: 991 square feet

Total Living Area: 2,594 square feet

Bonus Space: 532 square feet

Price Schedule: D

Width 50'-0"

Depth 53'-0"

An arched truss connects present and past above a 19th-Century style balustrade. Open living spaces play counterpoint to vintage bay windows with grille transoms.

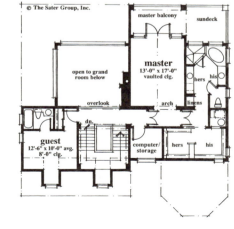

Rear Perspective

© The Sater Group, Inc.

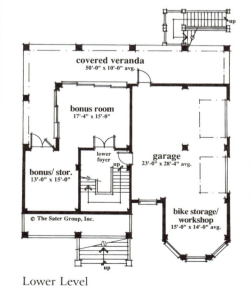

Lower Level

Main Level

Upper Level

396
Nantucket Sound

© The Sater Group, Inc.

The Sater Design Collection

Vintage seaboard details gently flavor this Nantucket waterfront plan, and convey a poetic symmetry that goes straight to the heart. A faux widow's walk creates a stunning complement to the observation balcony and two oceanside sundecks, together allowing panoramic views front and back. The raised, open living and dining area is defined by two pairs of French doors which frame a two-story wall of glass topped off by a graceful arch.

The spacious interior answers the call of the great outdoors with a bright *bon ton* of its own—warm, natural light and bountiful views. A cozy fireplace framed by built-ins invites gatherings of all kinds, from uproarious bashes to a little light reading for a party of one. A hard-working gourmet kitchen serves both family meals and planned events, with an island prep area, a walk-in pantry, a pass-through counter and its own French door to the covered porch.

Split sleeping quarters offer privacy to the main-level master suite. Upstairs, each of two pampering guest suites has a private bath with an oversized vanity and dressing area with a French door to the front balcony. A gallery loft leads to an computer area with a balcony overlook as well as built-in space for a desk.

Plan 6693

Main Level: 1,642 square feet

Upper Level: 1,165 square feet

Lower Level Entry: 150 square feet

Total Living Area: 2,957 square feet

Price Schedule: D

Width 44'-6"

Depth 58'-0"

Tilt turn louvered shutters and a reserved symmetry allude to island plantation houses, while timeless traditional graces open this home to the future.

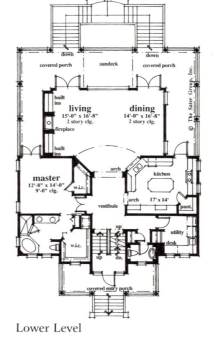

© The Sater Group, Inc.

Rear Perspective

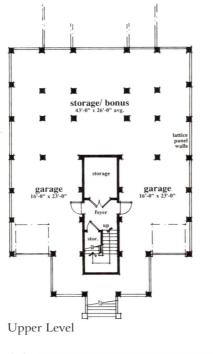

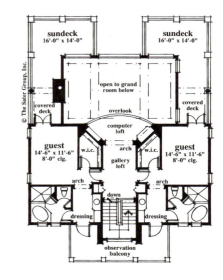

Upper Level

Lower Level

Main Level

558
Walker Way

© The Sater Group, Inc.

The Sater Design Collection

Lovely balconies and a magnificent circlehead window set off a three-story turret on this Gulf Coast design, perfect for a waterfront property. The staircase from the ground-level foyer to the raised living area enjoys elaborate views that make a powerful "welcome home" statement. Sliding glass doors open the great room to the main-level covered porch and sundeck, while a fireplace lends coziness and warmth.

A columned archway announces the elegant formal dining room, well lit by the bay's windows. Nearby, French doors open to a front balcony where gentle breezes can mingle with the glow and warmth of the interior. The gourmet kitchen is open to the morning nook, which boasts its own bay windows and seaside views. A single French door leads out to the verandah.

The upper level is dedicated to a spacious master suite and a private, bayed study. A corner fireplace warms both bedroom and bath in the homeowner's retreat. The soaking tub and glass-enclosed shower have views of the back property. Sliding glass doors open to the rear sundeck, while a morning kitchen serves juice and coffee near a front balcony.

Plan 6697

Main Level: 1,642 square feet

Upper Level: 927 square feet

Total Living Area: 2,569 square feet

Bonus Space: 849 square feet

Price Schedule: D

Width 60'-0"

Depth 44'-6"

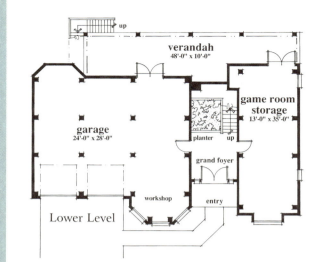

Lower Level

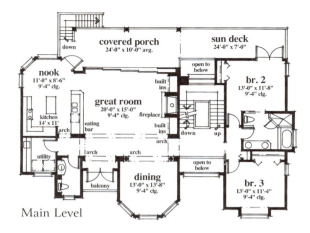

Main Level

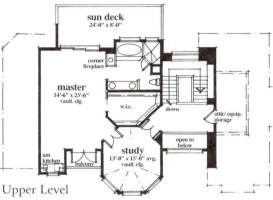

Upper Level

This stunning Gulf Coast cottage will be the prettiest house in the neighborhood. Wide windows take in gorgeous views, while cool outdoor spaces invite festive bashes, or just a little light reading.

© The Sater Group, Inc.

Rear Perspective

388
Wulfert Point

© The Sater Group, Inc.

The romantic Charleston coast is rich with the timeless serenity of quiet island communities, where a relaxed attitude is *de rigueur* and architectural styles blend to a folksy vernacular. This retreat is pure heaven, decked out with a Charleston Row courtyard with a sundeck, spa and lap pool. Louvered shutters and circlehead windows speak softly of the past, while French doors extend the living areas and welcome sunlight and balmy breezes inside.

An easygoing classicism flows from front to back, with gentle arches and decorative columns that announce interior vistas as well as multidirectional views. Three sets of French doors extend an invitation to the covered porch, sundeck and courtyard. A beautiful bayed formal dining room is open to the gourmet kitchen, which shares its views.

The second level includes two secondary bedrooms, which share a bath, and a grand master suite with walls of glass that bring the outside in. Double doors open to the covered balcony from the bedroom, while a bay window splashes the bath with sunlight. A bonus room over the garage has a morning kitchen and a full bath could be built as a home theater or office.

Plan 6688

Main Level: 1,293 square feet

Upper Level: 1,154 square feet

Bonus/Guest Suite: 426 square feet

Total Living Area: 2,873 square feet

Price Schedule: D

Width 50'-0"

Depth 90'-0"

A Bahamian influence lends a comfy, "real house" look and feel to this contemporary villa. The pure geometry of Old Charleston Row style is sweetened by a gentle Caribbean flavor.

© *The Sater Group, Inc.*

Rear Perspective

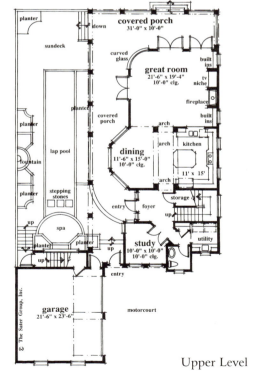

Main Level

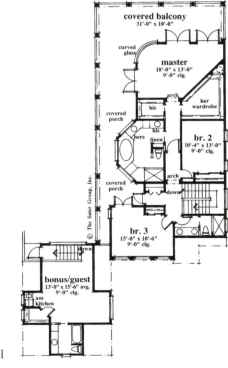

Upper Level

712
Southampton Bay

© The Sater Group, Inc.

A classic pediment and low-pitched roof are topped by a cupola on this gorgeous coastal design, influenced by 19th-century French Caribbean estate houses. Inside, versatile style and modern practicality blend to a relaxed atmosphere with both comfy niches and grand, welcoming arches. The beauty and warmth of natural light splash the spacious living area with a sense of the outdoors—and a touch of *joie de vivre*.

A stunning sunburst sets off the entry and announces the foyer's impressive, but not imposing, staircase. The great room features a wall of built-ins designed for even the most technology-savvy entertainment buff. Dazzling views through great walls of glass are enlivened by the presence of a breezy portico, set off by European-style arches.

The master suite features a luxurious bath, a dressing area and His and Hers walk-in closets. Glass doors open to the portico, offering generous views, while a nearby study provides an indoor retreat. A gallery hall with an art niche leads to two family bedrooms, which share a full bath. Lower-level space includes a game room, a bonus room, extra storage and plans for an optional elevator.

Plan 6684

Main Level: 2,385 square feet
Lower Level Entry: 80 square feet
Total Living Area: 2,465 square feet
Price Schedule: D
Width 60'-4"
Depth 59'-4"

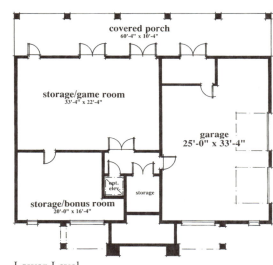

Lower Level

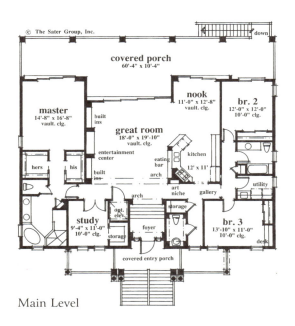

Main Level

© *The Sater Group, Inc.*

Rear Perspective

Caribbean architecture takes on a new attitude with this contemporary cottage. Savory comfort and blissful simplicity invite year-round living.

527

Tucker Town Way

The Sater Design Collection

The dramatic arched entry of this Southampton-style cottage borrows freely from its Southern coastal past. A muted tropical palette weds artful details that preserve its Atlantic heritage, creating a happy marriage of casual and traditional. The foyer and central hall open to the grand room, where a crackling fire is an elegant complement to wild breezes that waft through the spacious interior.

The heart of the home is served by a well-crafted kitchen with hard-working amenities. Wrapping counter space, a casual eating bar and a corner walk-in pantry please the cook, while the adjacent morning nook welcomes the entire family. An archway announces the elegant formal dining room, which features a box-bay window.

A secluded master suite offers access to the lanai through French doors. The bedroom leads to an opulent private bath through a dressing area flanked by His and Hers walk-in closets. A step-up soaking tub, twin lavatories and a glass-enclosed shower highlight the master bath. Two secondary bedrooms which share a full bath reside to the right of the plan.

Plan 6692

Total Living Area: 2,068 square feet
Price Schedule: C
Width 58'-0"
Depth 54'-0"

Triple gables add vintage Atlantic character to the modern presence of this coastal plan. Galleries open the interior spaces to gentle breezes, while recreation space adds room to grow.

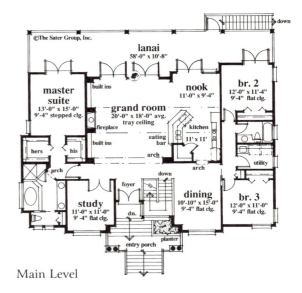

© The Sater Group, Inc.

Rear Perspective

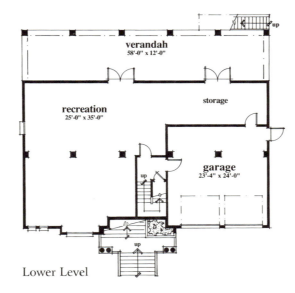

Lower Level

Main Level

253
Nassau Cove

© The Sater Group, Inc.

Classic clapboard siding sets off a metal roof and latticework fret detail on this island cottage. True to its tropical roots, this design features a raised living area announced by a symmetrical staircase and a balustered porch. An unrestrained floor plan offers both open, spacious living areas and well-defined sleeping rooms with outdoor views.

Double French doors lead to the rear deck from the grand room, which has a cozy fireplace. Both sides of the formal dining room open to decks, positioned to capture prevailing gentle breezes. The well-appointed kitchen overlooks the living area, splashed with the beauty and warmth of natural light.

Upstairs, a hall with a balcony overlook leads to French doors, which announce the homeowner's retreat. A morning kitchen conveniently prepares juice and coffee while a private observation deck invites sunning and stargazing. The master bath boasts a windowed, whirlpool tub, an oversized shower, two lavatories and a U-shaped walk-in closet.

Plan 6654

Main Level: 1,342 square feet

Upper Level: 511 square feet

Total Living Area: 1,853 square feet

Price Schedule: D

Width 44'-0"

Depth 40'-0"

© The Sater Group, Inc.

Rear Perspective

This Bahamian paradise is all decked out with lots of tranquil outdoor places. Wide windows capture grand views that satisfy a blissfully easygoing interior.

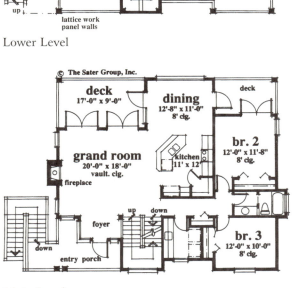

c The Sater Group, Inc.

garage
40'-0" x 20'-0" avg.

storage
13'-0" x 18'-0" avg.

stor./bonus
20'-0" x 20'-0"

up   stor.

up

lattice work
panel walls

Lower Level

© The Sater Group, Inc.

deck
17'-0" x 9'-0"

dining
12'-8" x 11'-0"
8' clg.

deck

grand room
20'-0" x 18'-0"
vault. clg.

kitchen
11' x 12'

br. 2
12'-0" x 11'-8"
8' clg.

fireplace

up   down

foyer

down

entry porch

br. 3
12'-0" x 10'-0"
8' clg.

Main Level

observation
deck

master
13'-0" x 14'-0"
vault. clg.

am
kitchen

open to grand
room below

down

© The Sater Group, Inc.

Upper Level

491

Abaco Bay

© The Sater Group, Inc.

The Sater Design Collection

Lattice walls, pickets and horizontal siding complement a relaxed Key West island-style design that boasts a spacious sitting porch. Sunburst transoms lend a romantic spirit to this seaside destination, perfect for waterfront properties. Inside, an elegant interior doesn't miss a step, with an open foyer that leads to an expansive great room, made cozy by a warming hearth. Just right for entertaining, the living and dining rooms open to the veranda, which even invites a moonlit after-dinner dance—why not?

A gallery hall leads to two family or guest bedrooms, one with French doors to the veranda. The upper level is dedicated to the master suite—a perfect, and private, homeowner's retreat. French doors reveal a vestibule open to both bedroom and bath. A sizable walk-in closet and a morning kitchen complement lavish amenities in the bath: a vanity with an arched soffit ceiling above, a dormered spa-style tub and an oversized shower with a seat. Enclosed storage plus bonus space is tucked away on the lower level.

Plan 6655

Main Level: 1,586 square feet

Upper Level: 601 square feet

Total Living Area: 2,187 square feet

Price Schedule: C

Width 50'-0"

Depth 44'-0"

Open rooms and vaulted ceilings lend an aura of hospitality to this waterfront cottage. A high-pitched roof and double porticos lend a casual, Key West attitude.

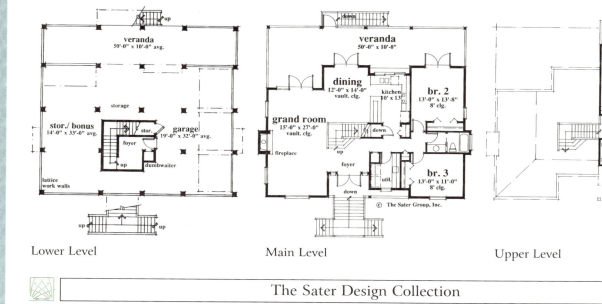

© The Sater Group, Inc.

Rear Perspective

Lower Level

Main Level

Upper Level

138
Runaway Bay

© The Sater Group, Inc.

The Sater Design Collection

Here's a seaside retreat with an easy-going style. This Floridian home is built for the kisses and kicks of a coastal climate, with a raised living area that invites sultry ocean breezes and allows distant views. Its relaxed attitude is carried throughout the home with carefully designed living spaces and soothing style.

A high-pitched metal roof highlights a striking exterior and complements horizontal siding, shutters and a charming staircase. The entry leads through a well-lit foyer to an expansive great room, warmed by a fireplace. Lovely French doors lead out to the screened verandah, also accessed from a well-appointed gourmet kitchen and dining area. A roomy sundeck hosts casual meals, morning coffees and afternoon teas.

Split sleeping quarters offer a secondary bedroom on the main level, plus a nearby study that shares its full bath. The upper level is dedicated to a luxurious master suite that features a spacious private bath with a knee-space vanity and a dressing area. Storage and bonus space surround an ample carport on the lower level.

Plan 6616

Main Level: 1,136 square feet

Upper Level: 636 square feet

Total Living Area: 1,772 square feet

Price Schedule: D

Width 41'-9"

Depth 45'-0"

This island-flavored Floridian plan offers a master suite with a lofty vantage point. The heart of the home opens to a screened verandah, served by a gourmet kitchen, for casual, outdoor entertaining.

© The Sater Group, Inc.

Rear Perspective

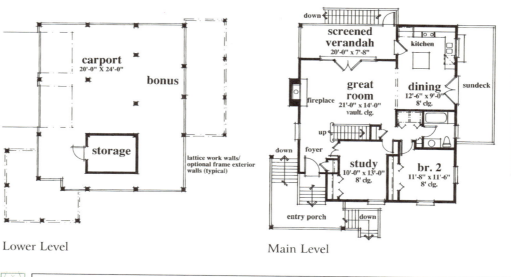

Lower Level

Main Level

Upper Level

Jenkins & Hinshaw

716
Tradewind Court

© The Sater Group, Inc.

This raised tidewater design features a steeply pitched metal roof that beats back the sun and reflects the traditions of the island tropics. But this charming two-story cottage home is suited for a myriad of building situations, with carefree and comfortable outdoor areas that encourage year-round living.

Deep overhangs above the entry and forward windows shield the interior from harsh sunlight. Two sets of French doors to the back of the plan open the great room and dining room to sea breezes and prime views, complemented by a cozy fireplace. A windowed double sink open the kitchen to views and sunlight, while a convenient laundry keeps the living area tidy.

The main-level master suite opens from the foyer through a vestibule that offers a convenient powder room. The home-owner's private bath features two lavatories, a separate shower and a door to a secluded area of the screened verandah. Upstairs, a secondary bedroom with a dormer window shares a full bath with a cozy loft or third bedroom.

Plan 6617

Main Level: 1,189 square feet

Upper Level: 575 square feet

Total Living Area: 1,764 square feet

Price Schedule: D

Width 46'-0"

Depth 44'-6"

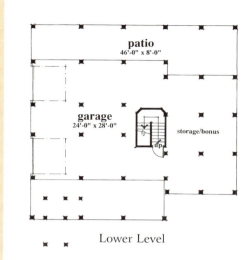

Lower Level

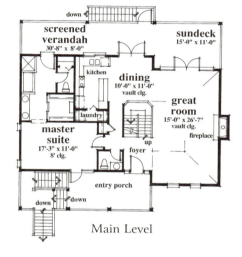

Main Level

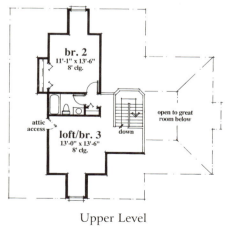

Upper Level

© The Sater Group, Inc.

Rear Perspective

Tradewinds turn to gentle breezes through the galleries of this raised tidewater design. A cabana bath eases the transition from sun, sand and sea, while the verandah invites the great outdoors.

© The Sater Group, Inc.

602
Admiralty Point

A true Southern cottage, this seashore design boasts a great, livable floor plan with room to grow. The raised entry is announced by a dramatic arch with a keystone detail. An expansive grand room offers a warming fireplace, built-in shelves and a great place for an aquarium. A wall of glass doors opens the home to coastal breezes and invites tender evenings of conversation on the columned lanai.

The kitchen offers service to a front-facing formal dining room, which enjoys natural light from a bumped-out bay. Ready for planned occasions and cozy gatherings, the dining room offers multi-functional space for active lifestyles. A corner walk-in pantry, an eating bar open to the grand room, and a windowed morning nook brighten the kitchen.

A secluded master wing opens to the lanai through double French doors. Two walk-in closets surround a vestibule that leads from the bedroom to a luxurious, irresistible bath. Dual sinks complement a glass shower and a windowed soaking tub. Double doors open from the foyer to a quiet study with wide views of the front property. Lower-level recreation space may be developed into a home theater, game room or hobby area.

Plan 6622

Total Living Area: 2,190 square feet

Price Schedule: C

Width 58'-0"

Depth 54'-0"

Wide, shady verandahs invite lingering in the best Southern tradition with this tidewater design. A seaside sensibility mixes high style with a kind of barefoot elegance.

Cost to build? See page 60 to order complete cost estimate to build this house in your area!

Rear Perspective

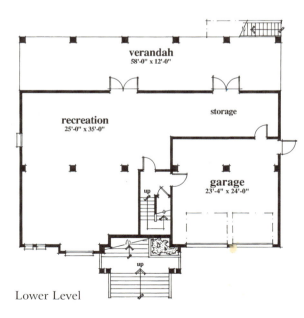

Lower Level

Main Level

315

Spyglass Hill

© The Sater Group, Inc.

Lattice panels, shutters and a steeply pitched metal roof speak softly of early Caribbean plantation style and add character to this island cottage. Infused with a tropical architecture, the design raises its living areas above ground level and allows trelliswork to add its grace notes to the charming exterior. A glass-paneled entry opens to a well-lit foyer and a grand central staircase which leads to the great room.

Lovely French doors transform interior space with a sense of the outdoors, and invite gracious entertaining on the verandah. An elegant dining room shares the glow of the great room's fireplace and captures views of the rear grounds through a picture window. The open stairway wall nearby offers space for a buffet or a china hutch. A well-appointed kitchen serves both the formal dining room and a glassed-in morning nook.

Upstairs, double doors open the sumptuous master suite to a private deck, and invite balmy sea breezes inside. Two walk-in closets introduce a grand bath that offers a windowed whirlpool tub, a double-bowl vanity and a separate shower. Two main-level secondary bedrooms accommodate guests and share a full bath.

Plan 6615

Main Level: 1,736 square feet

Upper Level: 640 square feet

Total Living Area: 2,376 square feet

Price Schedule: D

Width 54'-0"

Depth 44'-0"

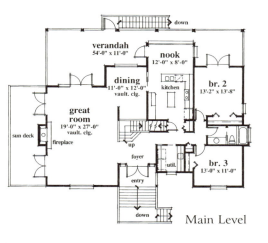

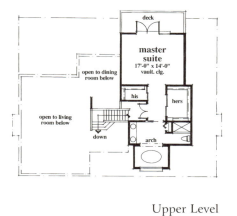

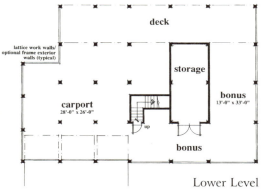

Cost to build? See page 60 to order complete cost estimate to build this house in your area!

© The Sater Group, Inc.

Rear Perspective

French doors and the glamour of glass take in gorgeous views and lend a light and airy nature to this tropical design. A roomy sun-deck and a verandah blur the line between outdoors and in.

Lower Level

Main Level

Upper Level

A portico-style entry is a warm welcome to this detached three-car garage, styled to complement any of the cottage designs. Bonus space above offers an additional living area or a recreation room. With a morning kitchen, a full bath, a vaulted ceiling and three dormered windows, Option A may developed as a comfortable guest suite or a charming artist's studio. The entry vestibule provides ample storage space as well as a wrapping stair to the bonus level.

Plan 6704

Garage: 770 square feet

Vestibule/Stairs: 137 square feet

Upper Bonus Space: 497 square feet

Price Schedule: G3

Width 47'-6"

Depth 22'-0"

© The Sater Group, Inc.

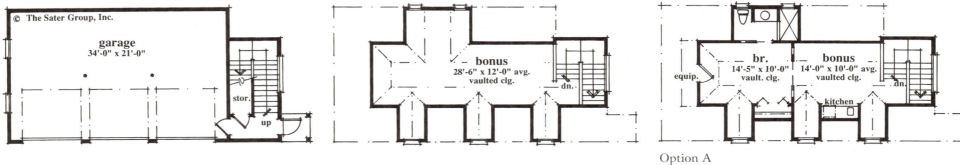

© The Sater Group, Inc.

garage
34'-0" x 21'-0"

stor.

up

bonus
28'-6" x 12'-0" avg.
vaulted clg.

dn.

equip.

br.
14'-5" x 10'-0"
vault. clg.

bonus
14'-0" x 10'-0" avg.
vaulted clg.

kitchen

dn.

Option A

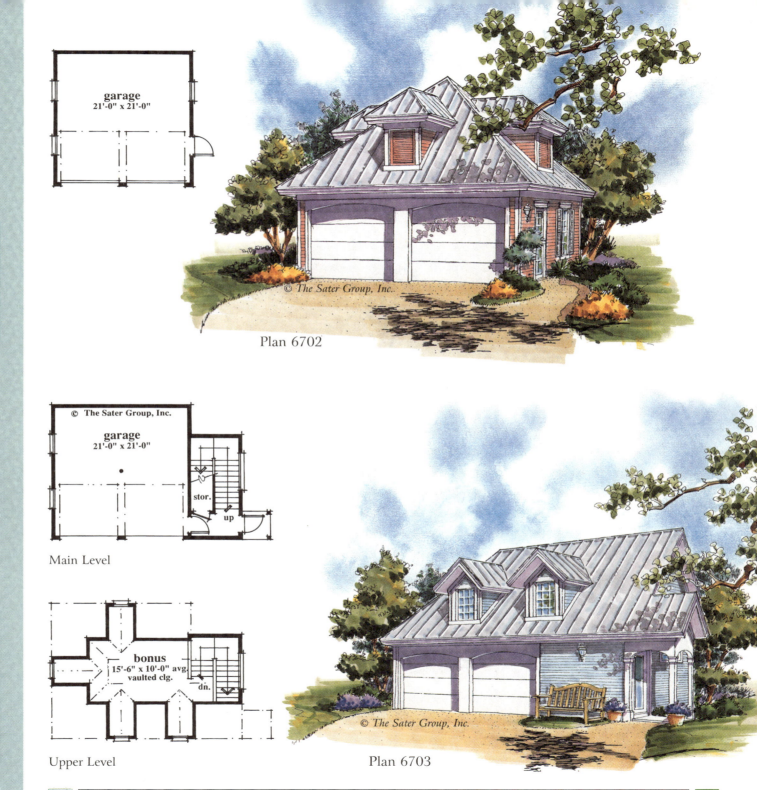

Vented dormers and a high-pitched, insulated metal roof dress up this two-car garage with quaint details that blend beautifully with any of the cottage homes. With three windows and a side entry, this garage is convenient and well lit.

Plan 6702

Square footage: 484
Price Schedule: G1
Width 22'-0"
Depth 22'-0"

garage
21'-0" x 21'-0"

Plan 6702

A roomy vestibule offers additional storage space with this stylish two-car garage. Flexible space above may be developed into a hobby/craft area, a home office or even an extra bedroom. Charming dormer windows allow views and cool breezes to enhance the bonus level.

Plan 6703

Garage: 484 square feet
Vestibule/Stairs: 137 square feet
Upper Bonus Space: 264 square feet
Price Schedule: G2
Width 34'-6"
Depth 22'-0"

© The Sater Group, Inc.

garage
21'-0" x 21'-0"

stor.

up

Main Level

bonus
15'-6" x 10'-0" avg.
vaulted clg.

dn.

Upper Level

Plan 6703

The Blueprint Package

Each set of home plan blueprints is a related gathering of plans, diagrams, measurements, details and specifications that precisely show how your new residence will come together. Each home design receives careful attention and planning from our expert staff to ensure quality and buildability.

Here's what the package includes:

- Designer's rendering of front elevation
- Foundation and dimensioned floor plans
- Building cross-sections
- Selected interior elevations
- Working drawings of ¼" scale or larger
- Door and window sizes
- Roof plan and exterior details

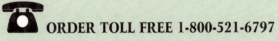 **ORDER TOLL FREE 1-800-521-6797**

After you've looked over The Blueprint Package and Important Extras on the following page, simply mail the order form on page 63 or call toll free on our **Blueprint Hotline: 1-800-521-6797.**

Important Extras To Do The Job Right!

QUOTE ONE®

SUMMARY COST REPORT/MATERIALS COST REPORT

A new service for estimating the cost of building select designs, the Quote One® system is available in two separate stages: The Summary Cost Report and the Materials Cost Report.

The Summary Cost Report shows the total cost per square foot for your chosen home in your zip-code area and then breaks that cost down into ten categories showing the costs for building materials, labor and installation. The total cost for the report (which includes three grades: Budget, Standard and Custom) is just $19.95 for one home, and additionals are only $14.95. These reports allow you to evaluate your building budget and compare the costs of building a variety of homes in your area.

Make even more informed decisions about your home-building project with the second phase of our package, our Materials Cost Report. This tool is invaluable in planning and estimating the cost of your new home. The material and installation (labor and equipment) cost is shown for each of over 1,000 line items provided in the Materials List (Standard grade) which is included when you purchase this estimating tool. It allows you to determine building costs for your specific zip-code area and for your chosen home design. Space is allowed for additional estimates from contractors and subcontractors, such as for mechanical materials, which are not included in our packages. This invaluable tool is available for a price of $110, which includes a Materials List.

The Quote One® program is continually updated with new plans. If you are interested in a plan that is not indicated as Quote One,® please call to verify the status. To order these invaluable reports, use the order form on page 63 or call 1-800-521-6797.

Construction Information

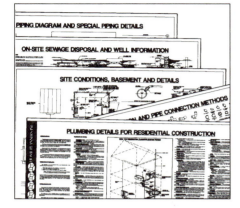

PLUMBING

If you want to know more about the complete plumbing system, these 24x36-inch detail sheets will prove very useful. Prepared to meet requirements of the National Plumbing Code, these six fact-filled sheets give general information on pipe schedules, fittings, sump-pump details, water-softener hookups, septic system details and much more. Color-coded sheets include a glossary of terms.

ELECTRICAL

Prepared to meet requirements of the National Electrical Code, these comprehensive 24x36-inch drawings come packed with helpful information, including wire sizing, switch-installation schematics, cable-routing details, appliance wattage, doorbell hookups, typical service panel circuitry and much more. Six sheets are bound together and color-coded for easy reference. A glossary of terms is also included.

CONSTRUCTION

To help you understand how your house will be built—and offer additional techniques—this set of drawings depicts the materials and methods used to build foundations, fireplaces, walls, floors and roofs. Where appropriate, the drawings show acceptable alternatives. These six sheets will answer questions for the advanced do-it-yourselfer or home planner.

MECHANICAL

This package will help you make informed decisions and communicate with subcontractors about heating and cooling systems. The 24x36-inch drawings contain instructions and samples that allow you to make simple load calculations and preliminary sizing and costing analysis. Covered are today's most commonly used systems from heat pumps to solar fuel systems. Complete with illustrations and diagrams.

SPECIFICATION OUTLINE

This 16-page document is critical to building your house correctly. Designed to be filled in by you or your builder, this book lists 166 stages or items crucial to the building process. It provides a comprehensive review of the construction process and helps in choosing of materials. When combined with the blueprints, a signed contract, and a schedule, it becomes a legal document and record for the building of your home.

11"x17" COLOR RENDERING

Full-color renderings suitable for framing are available for all of the plans contained in this book. For prices and additional information, please see page 62 or call the toll-free number listed below.

☎ To Order, Call Toll Free 1-800-521-6797

To add these important extras to your Blueprint Package, simply indicate your choices on the order form on page 63 or call us Toll Free 1-800-521-6797.

House Blueprint Price Schedule

(Prices guaranteed through December 31, 1998)

Package	1-set Study Package	4-set Building Package	8-set Building Package	1-set Reproducible Sepias
Schedule C	$430	$475	$535	$675
Schedule D	$470	$515	$575	$735

Prices for 4- or 8-set Building Packages honored only at time of original order.

Additional Identical Blueprints in same order ....$50 per set
Reverse Blueprints (mirror image) ....$50 per set
Specification Outlines ....$10 each

Exchanges ....$ 50 exchange fee for first set; $10 for each additional set
$ 70 exchange fee for 4 sets
$100 exchange fee for 8 sets

Garages Price Schedule	G1	G2	G3
One Set of Blueprints	$50	$60	$85
One Set of Sepias	$150	$160	$185

Additional Identical Sets (Garages Only) ....$15 each
Reverse Sets (Garages Only) ....$15 each

11"x17" Color Rendering, Front or Rear Perspective....................................$100
11"x17" Color Renderings Plan Set, Front & Rear.......................................$175

All prices are subject to change without notice and subject to availability. Reversed plans are mirror-image sets with lettering and dimensioning shown backwards. To receive plans in reverse, specifically request this when placing your order. Since lettering and dimensions appear backward on reverse blueprints, we suggest you order one set reversed for siting and the rest as shown for construction purposes.

Reproducible vellums are granted with a non-exclusive license to make up to twelve (12) copies for use in the construction of a single home.

Plans are designed to specifications published by the Southern Building Code Congress (SBCCI) International, Inc. or the Building Officials and Code Administrators (BOCA). Our plans are designed to meet or exceed national building standards. Because of the great differences in geography and climate throughout the United States and Canada, each state, country and municipality has its own building codes, zone requirements, ordinances and building regulations. Your plan may need to be modified to comply with local requirements regarding snow loads, energy codes, soil and seismic conditions and a wide range of other matters. In addition, you may need to obtain permits or inspections from local governments before and in the course of construction. Prior to using blueprints ordered from us, we strongly advise that you consult a licensed architect or engineer—and speak with your local building official—before applying for any permit or beginning construction. We authorize the use of our blueprints on the express condition that you strictly comply with all local building codes, zoning requirements and other applicable laws, regulations, ordinances and requirements. **Notice:** Plans for homes to be built in Nevada must be re-drawn by a Nevada-registered professional. Consult your building official for more information on this subject.

Index

To use the Index below, refer to the design number listed in numerical order (a helpful page reference is also given). Refer to the Price Schedule for the cost of one, four or eight sets of blueprints or the cost of a reproducible sepia. Additional prices are shown for identical and reverse blueprint sets.

To Order: Fill in and send the order form on page 63—or call toll free 1-800-521-6797 or 520-297-8200.

Terms and Conditions

These designs are protected under the terms of United States Copyright Law and may not be copied or reproduced in any way, by any means, unless you have purchased Sepias or Reproducibles which clearly indicate your right to copy or reproduce. We authorize the use of your chosen design as an aid in the construction of one single-family home only. You may not use this design to build a second or multiple dwellings without purchasing another blueprint or blueprints or paying additional design fees. The title to and intellectual property rights in the plans shall remain with The Sater Group, Inc. Use of the plans in a manner inconsistent with this agreement is a violation of U.S Copyright laws.

Modifications and warranties. Any modifications made to the vellums by parties other than The Sater Group, Inc. voids any warranties express or implied including the warranties of fitness for a particular purpose and merchantability.

Disclaimer

Substantial care and effort has gone into the creation of these blueprints. However, because we cannot provide on-site consultation, supervision and control over actual construction, and because of the great variance in local building requirements, building practices and soil, seismic, weather and other conditions, WE CANNOT MAKE ANY WARRANTY, EXPRESS OR IMPLIED, WITH RESPECT TO THE CONTENT OR USE OF OUR BLUEPRINTS, INCLUDING BUT NOT LIMITED TO ANY WARRANTY OF MERCHANTABILITY OR OF FITNESS FOR A PARTICULAR PURPOSE.

Purchase Policy

Your purchase includes a license to use the plans to construct one single-family residence. These plans may NOT be reproduced, modified or used to create derivative works. Additional sets of the same plan may be ordered within a 60-day period at $50 each, plus shipping and tax, if applicable. After 60 days, re-orders are treated as new orders.

We cannot honor requests for refunds but will exchange your entire first order for an equal number of blueprints at a price of $50 for the first set and $10 for each additional set. One exchange is allowed within a year of purchase date. **Sepias are not exchangeable.**

How Many Blueprints Do You Need?

A single set of blueprints is sufficient to study a home in greater detail. However, if you are planning to obtain cost estimates from a contractor or subcontractors—or if you are planning to build immediately—you will need more sets. Because additional sets are less expensive when ordered in quantity with the original order, make sure you order enough blueprints to satisfy all requirements. The following checklist will help you determine how many you need:

___ Owner
___ Builder (generally requires at least three sets; one as a legal document, one to use during inspections, and at least one to give to subcontractors.
___ Local Building Department (often requires two sets)
___ Mortgage Lender (usually one set for a conventional loan; three sets for FHA or VA loans)

___ TOTAL NUMBER OF SETS

Toll Free 1-800-521-6797
Regular Office Hours:
8:00 a.m. to 8:00 p.m. Eastern Time, Monday through Friday

Our staff will gladly answer any questions during regular office hours. Our answering service can place orders after hours or on weekends.

If we receive your order by 4:00 p.m. Eastern Time, Monday through Friday, we'll process it and ship within 48 hours. When ordering by phone, please have your charge card ready. We'll also ask you for the Order Form Key Number at the bottom of the Order Form.

By FAX: Copy the Order Form and send it on our FAX line: **1-800-224-6699 or 1-520-544-3086.**

☎ **ORDER TOLL FREE!**
1-800-521-6797

BLUEPRINTS ARE NOT RETURNABLE

ORDER FORM

HOME PLANNERS, A Division of Hanley-Wood, Inc.
3275 WEST INA ROAD, SUITE 110
TUCSON, ARIZONA 85741

THE BASIC BLUEPRINT PACKAGE

Rush me the following (Please refer to the Plans Index and Price Schedule on page 62):
___ Set(s) of Blueprints for Plan Number(s)_____. $_____
___ Set(s) of Reproducible Sepia(s)_____. $_____
___ Additional Identical Blueprints in same order @$50 per set $_____
___ Reverse Blueprints @$50 per set_____. $_____

ADDITIONAL PRODUCTS

Rush me the following:
___ 11"x17" Color Rendering(s) for Plan Number(s)_____. $_____
___ Specification Outlines @$10 each. $_____
___ Detail Sets @$14.95 each; any two for $22.95; any three for $29.95; all four for $39.95 (Save $19.85.) $_____
  ___Plumbing ___Electrical ___Construction ___Mechanical
  (These helpful details provide general construction advice and are not specific to any single plan.)
___ Quote One® Summary Cost Report @$19.95 for 1, $14.95; for each additional, for plans_____ $_____
  Building location City_____ Zip Code_____
___ Quote One® Materials Cost Report @$110, for plans_____ $_____
  (Must be purchased with Blueprints set.)
  Building location City_____ Zip Code_____

POSTAGE AND HANDLING	1-3 sets	4 or more sets
• Regular Service (Allow 7-10 days delivery)	$15.00	$18.00
• Priority (Allow 4-5 days delivery)	$20.00	$30.00
• Express (Allow 3 days delivery)	$30.00	$40.00
CERTIFIED MAIL (Requires signature) (Allow 7-10 days delivery)	$20.00	$30.00

OVERSEAS DELIVERY: Fax, phone or mail for quote

NOTE: All delivery times are from date Blueprint Package is shipped.

POSTAGE (From box above) $_____
SUB-TOTAL $_____
SALES TAX (AZ, CA, DC, IL, MI, MN, NY & WA residents please add appropriate state & local sales tax.) $_____
TOTAL (Sub-total and Tax) $_____

YOUR ADDRESS (Please print) (Street address required)
Name _____
Street _____
City_____ State_____ Zip_____
Daytime telephone number (____) _____

FOR CREDIT CARD ORDERS ONLY Please fill in the information below:
Credit card number_____
Exp. Date: Month/Year _____
Check one ❒ Visa   ❒ MasterCard   ❒ Discover Card
Signature_____
Please check appropriate box: ❒ Licensed Builder-Contractor
                              ❒ Homeowner

Order Form Key

TB56

Cottages

Book Designed by Matthew S. Kauffman
Set in Arrus and Caflisch Script
Illustrated by Jenkins and Chin Shue, Boca Raton
Composed by Tru Colour, Incorporated
Printed by Davidson Printing Company on Strathmore Beau Brilliant
Bound by Davidson Printing Company in twelve-point Carolina
Foil stamped by Larkin Industries in Foilmark #59